ALAN BIRKELBACH
NEW AND SELECTED POEMS

05

ALAN BIRKELBACH
NEW AND SELECTED POEMS

TCU PRESS
FORT WORTH, TEXAS

TCU TEXAS POETS LAUREATE SERIES

Library of Congress Cataloging-in-Publication Data

Birkelbach, Alan.
  Alan Birkelbach : new and selected poems / edited by Billy Bob Hill.
    p. cm. -- (TCU Texas poets laureate series)
  ISBN-13: 978-0-87565-340-2 (alk. paper)
  ISBN-10: 0-87565-340-5 (alk. paper)
  I. Hill, Billy Bob. II. Title.

PS3552.I7543A79 2007
811'.54--dc22

                              2006037459

DEDICATION
FOR LAURA, THE KIDS, THE GRANDKIDS

TaBLe of conTenTs

Introduction

Alan Birkelbach: New and Selected Poems is offered as the first book in a continuing line of publications, the TCU Texas Poet Laureate Series. When one thinks of previous state poet laureates, say Vassar Miller and Walter McDonald, the need for this project becomes apparent. I am honored to serve as its first general editor. I am also appreciative, as a Texan who tries to read what is important, for this series.

Alan Birkelbach is not a newcomer to the Texas literary scene. For some twenty years, he has been published in literary magazines known for their good editorial decisions—*Ilya's Honey, Grasslands Review,* and *Borderlands,* to name three. Anthology editors have picked up his individual pieces, and *New and Selected Poems* makes his fourth collected book of poems.

Birkelbach, a computer analyst, does not teach for a living. Not unlike Wallace Stevens, he never thought that trying to pay the bills with retail poetry was a sound idea. Neither professor of literature nor writer in residence, he measures his words, lines, and stanzas late into the night because he wants to, because he needs to.

He had read poetry, even before he wrote it. In *New and Selected Poems,* I see or hear stylistic and thematic echoes from a pantheon of American poets. In the imaginative "Robert Frost Among the Cannibals," Birkelbach praises Frost— "so talented of tongue."

Like Robert Frost, Birkelbach pulls images from the natural world—not that rural New England and rural Texas particularly match up. But in Birkelbach's poems, I perceive a keen craftsmanship like that of Frost's classics. Like Frost, Birkelbach can disguise a mosaic of word music in plain sight hidden inside conversational English.

Notice patterns of consonance, assonance, alliteration, and repetition in this brief final stanza of "Bewitched."

It's the liquid always journeying up,

pushing its foamy, rowdy way,

following the path of its own, clear voice.

Alan Birkelbach names a second popular American poet in another title: "You Should Be Here, Marianne Moore." Upon rereading both poets, I see one parallel. Marianne Moore's poetry often examines opposing forces in the thinking life. There is something of this in Birkelbach's poems. His opposites are not so much dilemma as in Moore's body of work; in Birkelbach's work, the opposites arrive as paradoxes. I am not sure if this balancing of opposites is engendered inside Alan's psyche—the right brain of an scientist juxtaposed against the left brain of the poet—but such a theory would partially explain this element.

In "Event, Clarity," probably an autobiographical poem, a couple flees their house during a power outage.

In Lubbock, in the middle of summer nights,

when the power would go out and the fans would die on us,

then we would remember the cast iron bed

had wheels, so we would creakily negotiate it

out the door and across the yard

and park it there in clear view of the road,

and you'd wear something flannel

and I'd wear faded boxers,

The poet then experiences a landscape of South Plains magical realism, where lingering solar heat yields to its lunar opposite.

The moon was an icebox cooling our eyes and cheeks;

it was white and pocked like a thin,

late Winter Texas snow

To carry my English teacher observations a bit further, sometimes a poem's premise involves unlikely, if not impossible, near opposites. In "Robert Frost and the Cannibals" and the surreal "Vincent Van Gogh Rode With LBJ One Day," such original concurrences are wonderfully set up and finished.

Of course, please enjoy this collection not for my reasons, but for your own.

With this project, TCU Press bestows upon the current poet laureate a book in print—an appropriately beautiful hardback—to honor his term. This series is hardly the first time that a university press has come through for readers when commercial houses have not. With *Alan Birkelbach: New and Selected Poems*, TCU Press makes a fine start.

I

You Should Be Here, Marianne Moore, To Explain This Mystery

THE MAN WHO MAPPED DESCANSOS

The fold in his felt hat
was as pure as a taco's.
He always tried to have
shined shoes.

He kept an old loose-leaf notebook,
where he had one page for each marker
telling about the day he found it
and what debris had been settled on it.

He felt that moving slow and deliberate,
driving always under the posted speed,
walking with straight shoulders to each
was what was wanted.

He knew that at the moment of tragic death
sometimes the soul stays around to be visited
and that when enough honor has been paid
then they will finally let go.

Ah, the descansos, the roadside markers for the dead:
Luis May He Rest in Peace
Always Missed
She is with the Angels.

He kept careful track;
one especially venomous corner had three crosses.
They were all unmarked but they were stone
and he wondered at first if they were an advertisement

for what, though, he wasn't sure.
He liked the wooden markers better because
they weathered well,
with fibrous wrinkles.

Each one had a smell he said:
most were flowery and sweet
but a few were kind of salty,
and some had a deeper scent

that made the back of his tongue curl up,
all sour and thick.
Here on the border road
he had filled a notebook this year alone.

His '65 Chevy with the bald tires
was always washed.
He felt like he needed to look good.
He imagined that, when he drove

with the windows down
he could hear low voices talking to him
because they all knew him
and they stroked his arms with the wind.

The one he liked best
was one he found that had
the rattlesnake skin wrapped around it.
He felt like that family understood.

Hueco Tanks

Yeats ephemeral scene does not square here
nor any husbandry that I know.
The urge to populate a venue
with delicate and verdant things
withers.

It would be a job to plow these stones,
to plant a boot. And it's no dolmen,
no Irish-rooted monolithic thing;
just a big squatting lump
with no alignment, no asterism.

Perhaps it is exactly all of this
that drove some ancient indigent sort
to crawl within the hidden crevices
              and paint so many furry-legged pictograms,
              whose arms were bristling with spears,
              or who were chasing things beyond the ken of years.

Perhaps it was hearing an indefinable music
              in that big sky
or being desperate to see a flower crack a seam.

Perhaps it was a yearning to capture something
and make it square, to burst it and find its heart.

Perhaps it was the search for the proper plow,
the perfect missing syllable.

YOU SHOULD BE HERE, MARIANNE MOORE

, to explain this mystery: a bird
has built his nest in that
mesquite tree yonder. Brave thing, or foolish more like.
Regardless, there's no feline that I
know gaunt enough to squander paws on a misstep.
Too chancy, too slick a bark,

too meager a mouthful for the trip
down. But more, what zephyr
led that bird through mealy, prickly maze? What secret
knowledge was it that guaranteed its
privacy, guarded fledging chicks? What fatigue of
wing? What urgency? What sight?

I saw a telling photo of you
once, Marianne. You were
bent over, furtive almost, standing beside a
herd of elephants, caught in the act,
listening, sagely private, learning ancient rhythms
that the most of us won't know.

I wonder, Marianne: If you joined
me, rocking, on this porch
would you dissemble, twig by twig, for me that nest;
would you describe gentle, grey footfalls;
or would you close your eyes, sigh, rock, and say, " ... how the
wizened boards sing, song, sing, song ..."?

POETRY, RIGHT HERE, IN THE CHUTE

It's my father standing there
with the big two-handed clippers,
and the other men pulling the chute together,
trapping the steer in place.

It's all the straight boards,
and all the boards notched or nailed.
It's all the steps, the ramps,
and all the leaning posts.

It's all the scuffed boots and overalls,
the cheap, straw hats,
the lingering smell of old coffee,
and the tested gloves.

And it's the sudden thick snip
as the horns are trimmed,
and the ears are notched,
and the blood starts spraying out

when the head tosses,
and the tongue goes thick and braying,
and the hooves stamp prints in the planks,
and the nose lunges in fear,

and it's a rite and a releasing,
and it's a slap and a yee-haw,
and it's a threshold,
and it's a never-ending christening.

WHAT'S IMPORTANT, AFTER THE STORM

The tornado that ate
through the yard that night
sanded the barn's side clear of paint,
carried off most of the chickens,

and, for good measure, toted
several of the stones capping the well,
flinging them with a bored shrug,
snapping tight fence wires like string.

By then we were in the concrete storm cellar
and we could hear the roar overhead,
ominous things we couldn't name
bouncing off the solid roof.

And we rode it out there,
in the darkness, flashlights
not bright enough to cut the noise,
the light making us too pale anyway.

That twister blew out fast,
like a cheap Christmas candle,
and we rushed up and out
to see what we could reclaim,

and Mom and Dad checked and marveled
on the house battered some but still standing,
and they started in to counting
what livestock was still left.

But all I could see, as little as I was,
was the grandfather live oak
that had held my tire swing
not an hour before

and there wasn't a leaf left,
just hoary, fibrous bones,
and its trunk was all twisted,
and its bark was rippled and layered like old skin,

and all its arms were pointed west and up,
and all its knots were molded into painful mouths
saying, "Sorry, but I held as long as I could.
Now your swing is up there—thataway."

wet water

God knows why it happened; it just did. Somewhere after sixteen hours straight of driving the cotton trailer things just kind of got unexplainable anyway. It would get so hot that dust devils would come up at night, gray ghosts that would spin across the sheared fields. The heat was smothering; after a while water couldn't cut the cottonseed dust and sweat built up on my skin like dark, wind-dried gypsum crystals. But I'd still have to wait at the gin while somebody sucked that cotton out. I smoked cigarettes, everybody did then, Camels if I could get them, Kools if I couldn't, and I watched the lifts carting the bales of cotton trying to find an empty spot in the lot. God knows why it happened; it just did. Some odd pocket of heat would get bundled up in that white burlapped fiber and just smolder. It might take hours, maybe days, but smoke would start curling out. The boss had posted a sign: Point out and move smoking bales immediately! Somebody'd shout and that lift would race over, grab that bale, and drop it in a big open area. Here's where you could tell the boys handling their first crop: They'd just pour water on the thing. A splash, a little surface soaking, and still smoke. Hell, plain water didn't do nothing. You needed the wet water, the heavy stuff, to soak down, to soak through. Somewhere after sixteen hours straight, at maybe three in the morning, the envy would set in for everybody You wanted to throw yourself under that splash, to feel that wet water, to feel clean all the way through, to somehow avoid that pending conflagration.

Tommy, the Man Who Broke Horses,

would talk about being all off the Earth,
his toes and the horse's hooves pointing down,

and he'd talk about the all-over getting quiet
when a body's not in contact with anything,

all quiet except for that one sound
that everything carries with itself,

its true sound, the sound it makes
when it is being just itself,

that sound from down inside
where the guts live and churn.

He'd say this and we'd say
he was crazy. One sound? We'd laugh,

and slap the dust from his shirt
but it was a look-away type of laugh

'cause we'd all heard it, that sound,
like thunder when it finally had intent,

or like that red squeal of the cornered javelina,
or like that shot-like strike of the rattlesnake coiled too tight.

Tommy, the man who broke horses,
would talk about the highest point of each buck,

and we envied him being suspended up there,
removed from all the squabble.

We longed to hear it; we wanted to know
what our sound was, to know if it was something deep and strong.

So, after we'd quit laughing, from a ways off
we'd squint at Tommy and envy his aches and pains,

and we'd talk to ourselves,
our mouths full of spit and yearning,

hoping something would give us the courage
to sit in that leaping saddle,

to give us the chance to fly,
to listen closely as we held on tight.

signs

If we'd listened we might have heard
some dread crows warning us.
If we hadn't been so full of sleep we might have seen
the sun come up behind black and green clouds.

Our horses, somehow, saw it coming first,
and tried to steer us home but too late then!
A slate-gray sky came down
and exploded on us with a sudden rush.

We closed our mouths and bent our heads
but that wind turned each seam and hidden fold.
Our boots turned into buckets.
Our brims fell flat against our eyes.

So we decided: We breathed once, deep,
then yee-hawed it, yipped and roared,
threw our heads back, foolish, daring,
slapped the reins, and cheered our horses to lather, set for home,

and laughed at all Fates that would drown us,
and washed ourselves with sopping bravado,
our horses' prints washing away in the mud
even as they were stamped.

We were cavalry leading a hopeless charge,
fearless of the spears of rain, the missiles of hail,
laughing and cursing that we hadn't scried the thunder,
but still looking up to read the twisting entrails of the sky.

Rapture

It will be like potatoes
in the rich loam of Central Texas
where you will be able to reach
with one hand into a furrow
and run your fingers around the clasping tendrils
and lift that buried thing up to the sun
and shake off the hanging dirt
like forgiven sins.

It will be like ghost crabs
tunneled in the South Padre sand
who feel the tremble of the truck wheels
and who barely have the courage to cast their eyes
out from their holes
to wonder at the thunder.

It will be like one night
on that vast Amarillo plain
when you wake up from a deep sleep
and you walk out onto your porch
to see the moon as a giant amber thing,
so deep and huge you could fall into it.

And out there, in the grassy field,
between you and that golden light,
are rabbits without count,
quivering with surprise and expectancy,
all wide-eyed wonder,
waiting like you, marveling,
at what has reached you in your earth-bound burrows,
at what has filled your ears and gaping mouths,
at what has pulled you up by your trembling roots.

RIGHT BEFORE YOU LEAVE EL PASO

going east there ought to be a kind of customs stop
where you are instructed to call to mind
all the songs you know
and sing them right into something sturdy.

Imagine that place:
"Here, Bobby, here's a candy wrapper, and, Sue, here's
a little extra room in a suitcase. Dad can have all the empty pop bottles
because he knows a lot of songs."
(And some folks, the ones who are poor and aren't toting much,
will be convinced to hum right into a paper bag,
or up their shirt sleeve, or into a shoe).

Imagine a Ranger grabbing Grandma by the ankles,
shaking all the tunes loose.
"We'd better not hear you singing out loud
until you at least hit Alpine.
We can't take your radios
but we'll be listening if you sing along ...."

Heading back south and east into the Rio Grande
the Big Bend doesn't tolerate much talking.
It's too big a place, too set in silence,
and all the people who have been here before have tried to fill it up.

But the Rangers say they can't tolerate any more nights
where the hot, humid wind carries pieces of old, foolish, brave voices
and impales them on the claws of the ocotillo and lechuguilla,
leaving torn shreds of songs
that weep and shriek and drift
from cactus to mesquite, from bush to thorny bush.

no Boundaries

We used to own a piece of the big hill
just west of Brownwood
before they put the good road through.

We would ride out to the point after dark
and look down over the town,
trying to identify everybody's house by their lights.

If it was nice enough, we'd let the horses graze
and we'd lay out a blanket. We could see the
drive-in movie screen at an angle,

the left side of John Wayne's face. The flickering
gray light would wash the parked cars.
We would imagine dialogue.

Or we'd just look out east, trying to catch
the stars rolling. If there was enough moon
we could see the clouds scud over,

right to left. He'd say, wonder where
they're going and I'd say, wonder
where they've been. There was nothing higher

than us except those clouds, and the moon,
and the stars, all of them moving beyond us,
and it made us always ask,

even though we already knew the answer:
Could even God completely grasp
a land as wide as this?

oklahoma storm

Emily Redfox scraped another sprig of sickly thistle
out from under the tomato-vine canopy,
then dug once more, slightly deeper,
to check for tenacious root.

She'd been reckoning by red-dust rivulets all day:
The sheening sweat beading waxy, speckled, pregnant,
bursting finally, swathing runes
through the dust on her arms, splashing her boots.

The moistness cooled, kept water on those internal slabs
of stone that, in turn, capped slathering lava
boiled from vials of demeaning tasks,
good-for-nothing-spouses, spoiled blood, white man's wishes.

Closer, she thought, closer still. Ah, there!
Another weed plucked by fickle, fateful blade.
Her hoe hissed on, kissed and scraped by tomato-vine whiskers.
Mrs. Birnbaum watched through shaded screen.

A breeze touched Emily's shoulder, chilled her arm,
kind of teased her lean leg, ran a wide hand down the tomatoes.
It was the only time since noon that Emily'd dared bend up.
She got paid by the plot, not the hour.

Through chain link, just in sight, Emily could see her plywood shack
sentineled by a cloud bigger'n'blacker than any mythic nigger:
A cyclone starting to descend—indiscriminate, lethal, on track.
Mrs. Birnbaum watched through shaded screen.

Emily thought: I should drop the hoe, jump the fence, grow wings,
get to the shack, pry the beer can out of his hand,
break his stupor, dodge his fists, close my ears,
drag him out the door, down the steps. Her arm wavered.

She thought again, felt the wind. Closer, closer still.
Too close now to beat the jaws.
Far enough away to miss the rip and tear.
A shadow filled the trailer's doorway.

A roaring filled her ears. She felt plates shift, exposed magma harden.
She surveyed the unhoed area, plotted a path, measured distances, costs.
She set her hands, her eyes, her lips, bent over.
Mrs. Birnbaum watched through shaded screen.

Knowing the Landscape

My cousin from Presidio always thought
lighthouses a strange thing

as if he didn't understand the ideas of
TALL and WARNING and

A PLACE TO AIM FOR IN THE DARK
which, of course, he did.

He knew West Texas wasn't the same as the ocean
and he was quick to admit it.

He would say he understood about warning ships
in storms but that wasn't the point, now, was it?

He was something of a fatalist I suppose.
He said he always knew where he was going;

he could drive the road from Presidio to the Big Bend
at night without his lights on and never veer from his lane.

If a man don't know the coastline, he would say,
then he shouldn't be at the wheel.

He had a logic I couldn't argue with;
it was inescapable and inexorable,

like the ocean leaving unconfident pieces
of wreckage on the shore,

like the mountains always coming
dead-on towards him in the dark.

HELD FOR THE BRIEF INSTANT FOREVER

There should be a relief of it,
something you can rub your hands over
so a blind man could know;
it should be tooled into a purse
or leather saddle—

but how to capture it?
How to make the kitchen clock stop
          when it never truly does,
how to capture the thrumming from the worm stick
that makes the nightcrawlers rise,

how to trace a new hoof print
and make it stay, lines fresh, untrammeled.
How can you do it,
what dies and stamps can you use,
what faith can you find in the leather?

How can you capture the steam from the stock tank,
a cottontail in mid-hop, the dog yawning,
the drumming thunder under a sheet metal roof,
the sun spilling over
and tilting the morning-glories?

What stitches can you use to bind the shapes?
What cut of the cowhide, what clasps, what bangles?
How can you make sure that
this moment does not escape you?
How can you hammer it in?

FENCE DUTY ON THE LAZY L

When the land had been firm
we had strung wire on those posts.

Now, during the drought,
our eyes could follow the lines of split soil.
Odd, we would say, how the ground would separate
in circles at first around the posts, like stacked rings,
and then start fingering off, large running cracks,
tiny earthquake faults.

We would scour for rocks and jam them down the holes,
make the posts upright, make the fence lie about
its strength.

Where there had been grass there was a memory,
along with any moisture. An overflowing well
was a dream. One man said even his wife's lips were dry.
My eyes opened more scratchy every day. All of our dogs
would bark raspy.

And every day that fence continued to fall, the ground continued
to craze. The earth would swallow the rocks;
we'd have to find more. Each day, driving up, we would see those fence posts
tilting like falling flags, poles we had righted
just yesterday.

So we would walk out through the dust, again,
pulling and jabbing and jamming,
thinking that in the pattern of the tilting posts,
in the writing of the mud hieroglyphs,
there had to be a message if we could only read it,
        or had enough faith.

Maybe if we could follow the perfect peeling track with our feet,
        or undo the correct twisted line with our eyes,
                then it might lead us to a bubbling well
                or the sky might reward us, yes.

But it didn't, and still we kept coming back, it was our job,
and everyday was the tilt then the pull,
        and the rocks so hot we could barely hold them
        before we threw them into the maw of the earth.
There was no answer in those baked pathways,
        no way out for our blind steaming faith.
It was a knot we couldn't untangle,
a path without a clue,
a dry labyrinth we couldn't escape.

EVENT, CLARITY

In Lubbock, in the middle of summer nights,
when the power would go out and the fans would die on us,
then we would remember the cast iron bed
had wheels, so we would creakily negotiate it

out the door and across the yard
and park it there in clear view of the road,
and you'd wear something flannel
and I'd wear faded boxers,

and you'd lay your head on my chest.
The moon was an icebox cooling our eyes and cheeks;
it was white and pocked like a thin,
late Winter Texas snow,

and we would watch satellites
drift overhead like determined fireflies,
watch them blink steady like breaths we had to take,
like our heartbeats measuring the length of night.

BINGO PARLOR, EL PASO

The women in the bingo hall have fat lips
too thickly covered with expired covergirl tawny rose lipstick
and those women clutch their daubers in sweaty fists
like each touch was making something gold.

And their husbands sit outside in the big heat,
and those men wear large belt buckles that say
Texas or that have tiny pictures of Elvis and Jesus,
side by side, hunks of burning love.

Uno, dos, tres, and so on, down the street,
little painted saints watch over the dried pools
and cracked weed gardens, and those saints
bless the cactus and the yucca and everything else left.

There is pear there on the cactus, pulpy, but no real meat
and the yucca, if broken, will yield a kind of milk, but thin.
If you squint just right you can see a Holy face
in practically any stucco surface if the shade is right.

And the game will go on well past sunset. Things are always
catching on fire here, and going out again. They work awhile,
then stop, come and go, like cheap prize toasters,
like a Tex-Mex sun, like money, like religion, like luck.

CORONADO POINTS

In Blanco County, near Floydada,
the man who lived in a nursing home
kept the chain link glove he had found over thirty years ago
in a box.

While probably important, he'd been told,
it didn't prove much of anything. It had less
conversational magnetism than a box of someone else's medals.
It was just something limp lying around.

It wasn't until folks started finding
copper crossbow points in that same canyon
where the old man had wandered
that someone who knew someone

dropped off a letter to an anthropologist
who right off said, "Coronado. Yes, I'd bet,
by God, he passed this way looking for that place,
looking for Quivira,

where there were huge boats and monstrous fish
and 'las platas de oro.'" That anthropologist,
when he heard, had to wipe his mouth.
"You wait," he said,

"people will be digging there for years
looking for more proof, looking for the trail."
A scanning hawk, that far-off day,
might have seen the falling glove's glimmer

or maybe he flew on, intent on prey in
the next canyon, or maybe that glove fell
across the path of a route-ruled rattler
who, envious of the fine scales, struck,

and then followed his natural track. Or maybe
someone should hurry back to that nursing home
in Blanco County, near Floydada, and find
that man who's still got the box,
and ask him quick, before he dies,

"Tell me,
when you first saw it lying there,
exactly which way
               were the fingers pointing?"

EL DIA DEL MUERTE

In that tepid tropical morning,
bathed by wafting smells of preservative spice and cinnamon,
she had sat alone on the terrace, drinking her sweet coffee.
Sunrise streaked, full of portent,
a lizard had darted up the flagstones
and stopped beside her chaise-longue
to stare at her with one baleful eye.
He had raised his fan, hesitated,
but he had forgotten his message
(or had chosen, more cruelly, not to tell).
He had hissed, then disappeared among the fronds.

Clammy, uneasy, leaving her husband still in bed,
she had gone to mass (in a Catholic church she had found
using the tourista map).
Afterwards he had joined her, barely smiling, at the parade
up to the garden and tombs.
It was there that he had said the word
divorce.
He had said the word, divorce, again,
(to make sure she understood)
and how he knew he should have said something before they came.

He never looked at her,
just kept his eyes on the mock procession,
the faceless figures, the passing food, the trinkets.
He had dropped her hand he had been holding.
She had tried to refocus; she had tried to count, between her feet,
as she continued to walk,
the smashed sugar skulls inadvertently dropped.
She had tried to imagine what those casings might have held before.

Unblinking, she had glanced inside the tombs and had felt envious.
She could see herself lying in bed, alive but cavernous inside,
surrounded by prayer-filled candles
creased fotografias.
She began to feel drier, stiffer,
not having to breathe, not having the disability of a heart.
Back at the hotel there is a garish fiesta, a ghoulish masque,
the waiters, dressed in skeleton costumes,
bearing death's-head multi-colored pastries.
She hears the churr, the ripping rattle, the hiss
of the papier mâché hair on the burro piñata,
So close she smells the wood of the bat she wanly winces
on each of his blindfolded, futile swings at the mindlessly

jerking, moving, spinning target.
She dully considers what that casing might hold.
Then, abruptly, the sudden smash, smash
and the spewing exhalation;
she looks down, expectantly,
fragilely aware of the omnivorous rushing for the scattered bits,
the sweet intestines.

WHEN THE BIG RAINS CAME

Once upon a time rainwater eroded the supports
of a concrete bridge that stood twenty feet above the water.
One whole section fell in, leaving a black, unmarked gap.
I wish this was the way an adventure began, a whole story:
Oh, look, there is a man driving his old truck
in the darkness along that road. No, there is road there,
his mind insists, but really he is falling.
He will have time to roll a window down and say "Hey?"
(Few people ever get that moment of suspension.)
In a breath the man will be floating down-river in his
fendered boat, for miles, maybe hours. He will finally
run aground on some exotic shore. And there he will meet a
princess who had been waiting, who had been
watching the dark, mysterious waters roll by.

BEWITCHED

Love is like witching for water.
You have to be sensitive enough
to see the things underneath:

like your wife's soprano floating like pie-breeze
through a window, the saint-white
of snapping sheets on the line,

imagining the aroma of soil when
it finally gets wet, the aroma of her neck
after you surprise her at the ironing board,

a heady draught of air here, a sigh,
sweat like sugar caught on the breeze,
a twitch in the hawthorn or oak.

It's the liquid always journeying up,
pushing its foamy, rowdy way,
following the path of its own, clear voice.

Autumn, at the River, After the Train Wreck

I was first.
I was the first one there. I was youngest.
I ran down the hill faster, propelled by my parent's shouts.
I knew this bridge, this river, this stretch of bank.
I had played here. I owned it. I knew the acorns and squirrels
and which rocks I could walk on.
I stopped and saw everything first, things nobody else would see.
I saw that metal snake dying, heard its final angry hisses in the water.
I saw the thrown boxes and books and boots and shoes.
I heard people moaning, still moaning, before they realized they could scream.
I saw people just there, and there, and there, and over there, quiet and still.
I saw, exposed by gouging, the red, sandy soil that
        I never knew lived underneath the gravel railroad bed.
I saw that somehow I had brushed against something;
        there was blood on my tennis shoes.
I noticed how the red color matched well, splashed on the maple leaves.
And I looked up track and down track and all up and down the river.
And I looked at the oaks and maples and all the rocks I knew,
and I saw that nothing beyond the "right here" of the wreck had changed much,
and I knew, all in a second, that it was both a small world and a big world,
and there, quickly, right where I was standing,
there was a sudden flurry of a warm released wind, a carrying breath,
that captured all the loose leaves scattered there around me
and blew them reassuringly, like golden, upward-flaming souls,
past my outstretched arms, my smiling face.

A PAINTING OF A BLACKSMITH

The right arm drawn back and over his head,
the left holding the tongs that bite
the metal rod, the fire-tinged thing,
waiting for the strike.

The focus of the eyes,
the set of the bicep,
the flat stance of the legs
and the solid, immutable grip of desire.

There should be a word
for the imagining of an echo,
for when that hammer hits,
when the need for shape is sent through an arm,

for when the hammer calls
and the hot metal answers,
and the clang and shimmers
go through the anvil into the boots.

This is the painting I want you
to dream of me at night:
the breathless gasp right before
the arm swings around,

the knowing that you need only touch me
and I will be hungry with fire,
that you need only call me
and I will ring red and sparking and true.

AS STONE

She would stop
hanging the clothes on the line
to watch him build
          the stone fence.

His stiff arms
lifting the barrow,
his pushing steps as sure and measured
as a pallbearer's,
the shoulders curling with the tilt and dump,
and then the rattle, roar and tumble
          of the stones, like heavy bones stolen from an ogre's cave.

He'd gone out clean
and grown dirty.
What a good word—grown.
She squinted a little.
He seemed bigger now,
slathered in soil and chips of stone,
sheened with brown sweat,
the barrow seemed small beside him.
She wished the wind would blow from him to her.
He was a golem, as solemn
and steadfast and holy
as any jewish-born statue.
She realized that her mouth was open
and that she was slowly pinching and unpinching a clothespin.
She knew he would come home later,
even darker than now,
all root and mineral,
skin-tone a myth,
bright eyes shining through a mask,
hands large and throbbing.
She didn't care as long as there was grit.
And she would meet him at the door
aching for redemption,
hungry to hold the magic,
searching for the mystic scroll
under his tongue
with her tongue.

I I
One Ultimate Telling Scansion

FaLLInG In

It's when something develops a hole unexpectedly
that you have to start watching.

It's not like the pinching and unpinching of a clothespin
she thought. When she bent down to the bag of pins
the blood rushed to the bruise in her cheek, making her squint,
making her focus more firmly on the thought.
It was like your grandma who one day is baking pies,
the juicy apple ones with the fork pricks for an edge,
and the next day she's just sitting pale and senseless
on the flower sofa
calling you by your brother's name, her eyes focusing on nothing.

One day you are twenty and your man stares so long at you
that it makes you feel uncomfortable and good at the same time
and every morning, yes, every morning, you wake up with him
and you can actually see definition on his delts and glutes
and you thank somebody, anybody,
that life is so nice and tightly strung.
Then, say, one day, he gets up before you get a chance to look
and the chain gets broken.
Maybe that fruitless mulberry in the backyard
is torqued by the wind just enough and now
instead of growing true and up
one limb twists and now there's a sumpy pocket that holds water.
Maybe some anonymous farmer when he climbed
from his field onto the road accelerated too fast on his tractor
in a dinosaur kind of way
and one errant tine from the rake dragged
all squimpy along the bar ditch,
making a line aching for erosion later.

One of her arms still hurt so she used the other one
to lift the weight of the sheet onto the line.
It's like a surprise; you can't plan for it.
You expect things to turn one way and for some reason,
this time, maybe from now on, they don't.
You keep the bugs off the tomatoes, you give them lots of water,
they look fine when you go to bed, and the next morning
there's a chasm big enough for a finger
and you can see all the veins and seeds inside.
One day you put too much sugar in the ice tea
or you don't iron the shirt quite right
and that open fist swings around when you aren't looking.

Weld, patch, concrete, fill, moan, pray, cry over it all you want.
The integrity of it's gone. So, what do you do?
You try to watch your step a little more but you know now
it doesn't do any good and why didn't anyone teach you this lesson, huh?
Wisdom sounds kinda like whimsy—but they aren't the same.
Next thing you know you are hanging clothes on a clothesline
working around the bruises.
Next thing you know a sinkhole
forms in the middle of a street and trucks start falling in,
water begins draining in that direction,
cool air starts blowing out,
people find bones at the bottom,
and at night the bats queue up.

IN THE MIDST, IN THE PATH, IN THE PASSING

When we were young and we moved into our first house
we christened the backyard by
making love among the jonquils.
I remember the hollow popping sounds
as we rolled an intimate swath,
only visible from above, at a higher distance.
Yesterday, when you were angry and threw the vase across the room,
I thought of when I was little and living in a trailer park,
when sissy was still around and Dad worked oil and Mom slept a lot,
and the tornado touched down one, two, three houses over and
bam, bam, bam they flew apart like firecrackers, but in a few seconds
it was over and only my hair was mussed a little, some drops on my face.
Things get spent and used up quickly.
Monks long ago measured time two ways: one, a wooden water bucket
with marks in particular places
(when the level reaches here then the hour is two past sunset)
(more and more erratic as time wore the grain), or
they used candles, cut a certain length, so big around,
to know that when it melted to a certain mark it was time
to wake another watch, time for prayers, for absolution.
Things get spent and used up quickly.
It is hard to see that moment when things change from slow, sensual and
soothing to something else,
sometimes hard to see, hard to accept,
but time does not change:
the erosion of water, the consuming flame, the destructive path
are only different facets and after-phases
of the stirring emotion I still feel when I look up into the cyclone
and watch
as it caresses and strokes the clouds it lives with
and knows so well.

FINDING A WOODEN LEG IN THE ROAD

It did not seem like
something that should be lost.

It was too perfect a thing, bondage gleaming and attached,
grain swirled and jointed,

all carved toes and painted nails,
nubbed, worn and chipped up to the calf.

It rested quietly against the curb,
not drawing attention to itself,

like a tired can or beaten newspaper;
my eye had just happened on it as I walked.

It was as heavy and strange to my hands as a step-child,
full of ghost aches and pains.

Had it fallen from some careless pickup loaded with miscellany,
(perhaps a theft from some house, grabbing all unsecured items)?

Did someone cavalierly toss it aside because he had extra,
because there was a newer model, more life-like, more attractive?

Was there dancing in the middle of a wish-filled night,
as that lost limb, like a lizard, grew back?

Had someone adopted a leaning life,
now bound to long skirt and overcoat instead of a foreign stick?

Or, if I listened closely would I hear,
a block or closer away, a rhythmic scuffing

as of someone fretting on his overworked heel,
wondering, wondering ....

The Former Poet Laureate Said

That he had finally just had enough
of admirers puttering down the sidewalk

onesy, twosy, like lost flagellants,
with copies of his books in their hands.

They were always mewling and whiny, waiting
for him to appear on his stoop

to "bless you, bless you all."
He admitted he was too accessible.

When he was younger inspiration
was as common as meatloaf.

He could pretty much rub two sticks together
and make a poem out of it.

But the reality was that one day his Muse
died inside him and he was left to try and hold

his reputation together on momentum alone.
It wasn't, he said, so much a matter of losing control

as having control getting up and taking a flight
one-way to Bolivia or some other godforsaken place

where it's probably struggling right now
inside some mustached coffee-picker

who owns one shirt and two goats and whose
entire vocabulary rhymes with "sangria."

But I noticed that even as he talked
he worked the chicken on the grill

and between the turning of each breast
there was an unspoken, counted pause

and the lines were laid in regular rows
that he would constantly write and rewrite.

DrIFTInG

Today a ghost crab floating alongside the port bow
will be your Christ, draped in royal kelp,
pointing the way to shore.

Yesterday it was a dolphin who swam beside the boat,
a gray, speeding blur who never checked to see
if you were really following.

Or maybe both are demonic incarnations;
maybe you are being led backwards up Dis,
maybe the water is the reality

and the times you used the astrolabe futile and foolish,
but a man's got to choose,
got to follow something.

The sea gives you a destination, an end point,
but you can't say it, have to accept it on faith,
drifting on that edgeless bowl you start looking for signs

like staring gulls or benign, guiding leviathans,
or unreadable patterns written in choking seaweed;
you get desperate to read a prophecy about your fate

about what waits for you when you land,
about what you will say, how the cargo will weigh out,
what face will Christ wear when you get there.

You expect confession and redemption when you land,
you want it, you need it, you dread it,
let it happen, let it not happen.

Maybe you should nod asleep at the rail,
slide overboard, not splash or paddle,
maybe it will be a falling longer than you know.

Maybe you should grip the wheel harder, aim for the reef,
yearn for the crashing and tearing, famished for the finale,
not wanting to go there but not wanting to tack away.

DIrecTIon

Everyone needs a good compass.
The old people understood it:
       "Align those stones so the stars have a voice in our lives.
       Drop them in place then count the days of winter,
            That direction will be East and that way West
            and that way South and
            that way ...."

But this is bigger than a North Pole thing, or lodestone, or magnet;
it's a pulling that urges our blood.

Remember how whenever Mama would set the watering can down
       the spout would always point a certain way,
           as if she knew which way
           the rain clouds were coming from?

When you play cards you and your partner
       should line up with the bathtub.
       It's the way the luck runs—downstream and flowing;
       stand alongside it, reach out, touch it, taste it.

Where have all the hood ornaments gone,
       the metal faces, the wings, the rockets
       those prows that arrowed us down the road,
           those perfect chrome and amber things
             that even if you were lost would declare
             "This way is the best way, straight ahead?"

Everyone needs a figurehead, a thing that leads you
       through the stinging, blinding water,
some unshakable needle that allows you to be

Babe Ruth, that lets you point your bat and say
"There. Up there. I am going to hit it there."

THE SEPARATION OF THE SEASONS

I have begun to think of you as a pumpkin
       and that frightens me.
I dread that there must be a cut, drying, green vine
  somewhere close by   yearning.
I know that this is way we used to sleep
  but I can't lay my ear on your chest anymore
  because I will hear the faint wind moving
  the moist, fibrous strings and seeds aside.
I think that one day, or maybe two,
  I won't remember to look
  but when I do I'll find your cheeks shrunken,
       more and deeper furrows around the cavities.
If there were room for a candle
       it would be burning low.

This season is too long.
I wish for the chill of Winter for you.
I cannot stand this long, drawn-out octobering.

EATING OR BEING FED

Robert Bly one year tried to not get out of bed
until he had written a poem. Easy enough for the prolific
and certainly staying in bed is a fine enough thing,
waiting for the Muse to serve breakfast.
I tried it only once,
but instead of birthing poems I ended up like
a man in the desert with a broken leg, gnawing on cactus.
contemplating thread count,
reading what I could reach on the headboard,
condemned, finally, to the horror of local television.

I couldn't get past seeing over and over
this Hispanic woman whose stepson soldier was killed overseas.
Oh and oh and oh she said again and again I blame the President
I will never forgive him forgive him forgive him
for putting my boy in harm's way
I noticed that somehow between the morning and afternoon news
she had found time to have her hair done
and she had obviously expressed her grief by buying a different
eye-liner color for every interview she gave.

Some people should stay in bed and some should not.
We draw our sustenance from what
we are able to crawl toward.

During one interview I got a glimpse of the soldier's father in the background.
He was busy digging some type of trench
in his backyard. He smiled once, waved at the camera,
made a V with his fingers.

A BOWL

He carves the kisii stone with the assurance
of someone carving wax. The curls fall back
on his stationary hand; they are cream-colored,
almost albino against his black skin. *Here,* he says,
this elephant is good work, buy this dark one, the one
I am working on, not that light one, that one
does not match your eyes. Instead, though, I favor a large bowl,
purple with many waving lines, soft and warm to
my touch. He smiles, says, *yes, that bowl,*
I think it has been waiting for you. Why is that, hey?
He puts down the elephant he has been working on.
He puts both my hands inside the bowl
and wraps his flecked hands around them.
Ah, there it is, he says. His eyes glisten.
He gives me a good price. I hold my treasure against my body.

I decide I will write a poem about him
I find out later—kisii stone is also called soapstone.
Anyone can carve it, even a child. There is no skill
involved.

       Everyday when I wake up,
or when I come in from work, the bowl is there, waiting.
Ah, there you are, I say. If I step closer the warmth
washes over me.

       When a poet friend drops in unexpectedly
       I feed him fruit and nuts from the bowl.
       Ah, there you are, I say.
Let's trade poems.

ASÍ ES LA VIDA

Tonight the Tarahumara will offer another sacrifice
of rabbit and corn, the meat divided
in meager chunks, the entrails
laid on the ground and stirred with a stick,
the bones and corn powdered and held up to the wind.

The next day, in the shade, under the still straw hats,
the size of the rabbit will be discussed
and how the corn was not as sweet,
(it must have been planted in the wrong phase of the moon
but no one believes that anymore).
A logging-truck driver will stop and talk a drunken braggadocio
about his many dollars from his crops
(from his hired hands) of opium and marijuana;

he knows lawlessness,
they know lawlessness,
the sun-washed stone walls
do not think much about lawlessness.

This is time as the Sierra Madre measures it:
the loss of grazing grass,
the fewer animal tracks by the thin streams,
the roar of insatiable saw.

The Tarahumara lie awake at night
and count satellites.
It is something they can do, like talking, or a sacrifice.

The valleys are still as deep here in the Sierra Madre
but the mountains are smaller.

JOHN THE BAPTIST'S HEAD

Again it happened
Some people have the knack and wrist for it but I don't.
It's tough to plan for a night like this when you know the script
and have played it before.
You can't impress a guy with a bottle of wine with a twist-off lid,
you have to get the real stuff, something with French words on the label.
But now, like too many times before, I'm gonna take too long getting into the
bedroom and he'll wonder, from where he's horny and waiting in the bed,
what the clanks and tinks are coming from the kitchen
while I pry the stubborn bits of broken cork out of the bottleneck
with the corkscrew, table knife, toothpick,
or any other pointy kitchen gadget I can get my hands on.
Finally, frothy, and almost ardor-less, I will show my face
with two wine glasses spiced by hints of chewiness,
and flecks of cork scattered across my teddy.
By that time he'll already be turned over to ESPN
watching synchronized swimming or curling.
The cutting off of the head can make all the difference.

My father took me bird hunting once.
He sighted down the barrel of his .22
and brought down a dove, one-sure-shot, bang.

There it was not quite dead at my feet, a splayed flurry, a gray duster
As I bent down to take a closer look at that round black and yellow eye
my father was quicker.
He said to make sure it's dead you twist the head off—pow!
So quick as spit he sure enough did, he twisted that head right off and threw it,
eyes, beak, and all far out into a field, no last chirp there, nosiree.
It made me wonder what I had missed, what notes were still unchirped,
what final sight was burned into that avian retina?
But I had Barbi's to play with later
        and wouldn't Mom like it if we picked these flowers?

The best beheadings are the unplanned ones, not like the French revolution.
No real surprise there for most of those frogs;
       they saw it coming, heard the rabble,
       figured it was for them, waited too long to finish their cake.
When those heads came off there weren't any questions,
No big whys caught in foamy red spit bubbles.
No "Hey! No! Wait!" sounds splattering around.

No, no, no.
(and you must understand that it's taken several broken corks
for me to grasp this),
the best beheadings are the ones where the cut-or, as it were,
has a deeper sense of why the thing is done but the cut-ee, if you understand,
is caught by surprise. Otherwise it's just a temporal mess
and everybody gets bored. It's like catching fish.
We sit there smug and secure with our mylar rods and stainless steel reels
and we relish in the name-sounds of our jimmy-flingy-tail lures
and we sing 'here a minnow there a worm' and we gauge the wind and depth
and we say he'll be right there splash and that bass only has a second to gasp
any fishy thanks he knows for lunch dropping right in front of him
before he is lip-yanked and dragged out of home.
He ends up lying on the bank,
looking for all the world like some drowning man about to speak,
gasp and gill and error,
and you're tempted to lean up close to him to see if those moving jagged lips
are trying to speak.

When you go to a lodge sometime listen to the sportsmen talk—
but keep in mind they're lying.
It's not the size, or the thrill of the hunt,
that makes them mount their trophy up on a wall.

So, a newspaper I read the other day said that somebody
had broken the seal in a tomb and found
the head of John the Baptist sitting on a platter.

How perfect! How mysteriously droll!
Maybe after the guards had batted the head around a little
with their scaled boots then Salome might have grasped that dripping thing
and kissed it with a caressing tongue because it's mouth was still in full shout
and it's eyes still sparking with some type of lingering fire,
but she only did it, and only would have kept it,
because she understood the timing of it,
how you have to be smart enough to know the questions,
how you have to be right there to catch the answerer—unawares.

That is why this man snores on my shoulder and I watch the scores.
I have not yet learned
the proper way to set the hook, to purse the lips,
to turn the wrist.

LIKE RAT-TAT-TAT-MARCHING CLOCKWORK, PACIFIC, CENTRAL, OR GREENWICH MEAN

I'm sure it's not as simple as these twenty-one lines attest but there it is—
it says that Ivan Dragitchjavic of Bosnia will once again be visited by the
mother of Jesus tonight as he has every night right at 6:40 P.M.
regardless of where he is in the world and that a service is planned tonight
at 6 P.M. at the Athletic Field House and that he will certainly have another
visitation tonight and I just have to ask exactly who we are talking
about here. I mean, I personally know a Jesus who drives a low-rider pickup
with a fuzzy dashboard and I'm pretty sure that his mother won't be there
because she's working for a nickel an hour in Nuevo Laredo making boots
and then there's that great invisible Jesus that my racist grandmother used to
call out to Sunday afternoon when Gale Sayers would be rushing for another
touchdown and my grandmother would cheer for any team he was playing
against and she would scream "Stop him Jesus Stop Him!" but his mother didn't
seem to be listening cause Jesus never did tackle. Or maybe that ain't the real
concern here because I have to wonder if 6:40 P.M. is maybe some mystical
time, like an equinox sort of, and how exactly does the mother of Jesus know to
change with the time zones, does she dial some mystical time and temp or wear
a lot of watches? But no, I'm thinking that sometimes places are haunted
and sometimes people are and that Ivan is from Bosnia and I'm betting
that every time he sees that Holy Vision he also sees buildings shattering
in a bloody slow motion and he's in awe of the fire from flashing phantom guns.

Lines WriTTen

Whenever someone visits that I rarely see
I ask them to carve their name, and the date,
into the large live oak in my back yard.
It's hard work, a big favor;
I tell them initials will do.
It would be callous to say
that the tree doesn't mind.
But the cuts are few, really,
and I never prune.

        Letters arrive weekly in my mailbox
        from other poets, poets I never get to see.
        Listen, your message has arrived.
        Your stationery was beautiful;
        do you want me to save it?

Go outside and look up.
Scratchings from years ago are now higher and expanded,
grown beyond arm's reach.
I went out one day and a branch containing a name I knew
had fallen dead on the ground. I wondered if it was a sign.

        Addresses are always nouns,
        have you ever noticed?
        There should be more verbs.
        Or infinitives.
        Some letters arrive yearning with forevers.
        Is one stamp enough for always?
        Can you hear me? Does someone understand?

Here's the knife, now.
Yes, we can talk about the other names if you want, but later.
This is our conversation, but not ending here,
or even after you carve, or at the gate
when we say good-bye, have a good trip.

> When I write back here is my reply:
> I have read your poems again yesterday
> while I sat under my tree.
> Wind shook the branches, making an acorn drop.
> I will let you know what grows there.

NAM ET IPSA SCIENTIA POTESTAS EST *

There is a place for what is muscular, like Hoover Dam,
unthinking and powerful, a slab of concrete for a face
      (like an all-State half-back named Tully or Max or Bama).

Sometimes when my father was hammering together
one of his many projects he would pull a nail out of his apron,
look at it, look at me, then toss the nail over his shoulder.
"Out of tune. I could tell by looking."

There will come a day when something small and perfect just happens.
You might sit at a stoplight, idling, when something tells you
to look at the driver in the next car. It is a woman, who looks back.
She will smile at you like your mother would smile.
Instead of speeding to work now you will drive slower.
You will carry that smile with you, wonder at it over coffee,
pull it out of your pocket during boring meetings.

It took me a long time to understand
the difference between the hammer and the nail.

I finally got it the day I stood on Hoover Dam
and heard the mindless roaring of the turbines and the water.

The tour guide made us bunch up, so close together I could barely breathe.
Finally we had to stand sideways, like vertical cordwood.
We tilted our heads back, opened our mouths, trying to get a breath.
Belt buckles and boots became weapons for space. I saw a laughing family,
not a part of our group, over to the side. They had a small child.
He was reaching with one perfect hand toward one escaping perfect balloon.
And the water behind them was blue,
so blue.

*Knowledge is more than equivalent to force, or, more simply,
Knowledge is power

on not seeing the lunar eclipse

Here in the night on the cold sidewalk, barefooted, full of sleep,
the sky is full of clouds and I realize I will not see anything,
certainly nothing as real and absolute as a lunar eclipse.
I consider going back into bed to my husband.

Instead I delay, tilt my head back,
and slowly spin in place in the middle of the street,
hoping I am looking in the wrong celestial location,
looking for an excuse for not seeing.

I look up and down my block:
I am the only fool outside looking at the stars.
Or at least the only public fool.
But that is maybe what I am.

How cozy to be in bed sleeping,
to be oblivious to alignments,
to be unaware of paths followed,
or how things shine—or not.

I want to call out, call out loud,
rattle on doors, slap on sidewalks,
run back into my house,
open my closets and scream into the back,

into the clothes that used to be me,
and say, "Remember when we all believed
that all paths were so sure?
Remember when we loved so brightly?"

But instead I realize my feet are getting cold
and the clouds are not going to move.
That thing that is vernal and pagan inside me yawns
and reminds me that I like

someone's warm hands holding me in place.
I teeter clumsy, chilled, and small back to my door,
savoring, even as the night closes away,
that last passing between things,

knowing even in the dark I will know where to go,
and I will have the memory of things
I can no longer see,
the memory of a brightness that is obscured.

ON THE PATH TO THE MAYAN PYRAMID

Santiago sits on an anonymous cane chair at the start of the path.
His large, yellowed front teeth overlap. He does not wipe his sweat.

A bat, small, with little character crawls down from his shoulder,
spiders down his arm and sucks the fig held in Santiago's fingers.

The bat smacks noisily, looking up occasionally at visitors who have
come to take a picture and maybe leave a dollar or another fig.

Santiago can laugh and cough (the moisture is thick) but he does
not talk. He is too picturesque. He does not mind the cameras,

neither does his little friend, who maybe has forgotten how to fly.
But many white Senoritas, Aiyeee-ha-ha, many do not go past him

to see the temple for when Santiago laughs, (and he laughs often),
they see his face and his fiber-caked teeth and they see deep into

his throat and they cannot see bottom but they know that there is
something hot and old and blood-hungry down there and they turn

their heads away and they hurry back to the hot, comforting bus, and
they try to wipe themselves clean

with their very white
and very new handkerchiefs.

THE man WHO DIDN'T mean TO TAKe AWAY MY FAITH

The man who fell down a hill and hit his head
told me he still had dark places where clouds seemed to have drifted into his
memory
and stayed.
It wasn't that the whole incident was gone.
There were moments of intense shade, he said, where, if he dared to look hard
enough,
he might be able to painfully see what had occurred.
"The cat in the box, the falling tree in the woods,
the monster under the bed theory, eh?"
and he slapped me on the back trying to laugh it off.

But he was hyperbolizing total darkness.
I knew he meant the nearly dark,
not liked a closed book
or Christmas decorations put away in a trunk.
It was more that hollow center feeling
when you put your son to bed, kiss him,
turn out the light,
but even with a nightlight all you can see
is the vague shape of the bed
so you turn the big light back on just to make sure your son is still there.

Or like that first time when you were young
and you made love under the arms
of a secluded tree,
and then, after the small talk, you got dressed to go,
and something kept making you look back
to that dim spot for keys, change, your wallet,
for any small piece of innocence
you might have left behind.

I KNOW A WOMAN WHO LIVES ON HARBINGER STREET.

I don't believe that I could do it
but she seems a pleasant and well-balanced woman,
not prone to starts or fits.
If it was me living on a street named that
I would be constantly peering
through the curtains to see
what cowled and ominous figure
was coming up the walk.
I would distrust all mail.
I feel sure that my newspaper
would always land grim headlines up,
crushing my bushes.
Anyone who drove to visit me on that street
would tend to get flat tires
and black cats would constantly infest my yard.
If it was me.
On a street with that name.
But, as I said, this lady seemed normal enough,
no twitches or flits.
Yet, then again, I noticed
that she had a little bobbing-head Virgin Mary
set up on the dashboard of her car
and with each bump and lurch
she would smile reassured as that icon would
bless her bless her bless her.

DISCOVERING THE MURDERED BOY

A rude step there.
A mumbled apology.
It might have been a nap disturbed.

Then I hesitated
and kicked this time on purpose,
but with care.

I did not want to find this treasure.
I shouldn't have, but I bent down
and ran my hands along the eyelets of his shoes.

Each of them were eyes
staring at me, wanting me to not call out,
telling me to move on,

to lie, to say my trail was blank,
to not make others see
how everything was unzipped and ripped and open,

all colors fiercely coalesced.
Everything too much blue and green and red
and white, white like old house paint,

white and spotty like birch bark,
white and purply like grapes in milk,
white like my lips as I patted his leg.

This keen decisiveness impaled me.
It was too harsh a statement, too little an obscure thing.
I would have preferred something else:

Me, fishing alone, counting dragonflies—
a far-off splash, an anonymous, drifting canoe,
a frayed rope trailing in the water ....

LIKE THE MOTHER FINDING HER DAUGHTER'S BABY IN A DRAWER

Perhaps she was only searching for socks
or a lacy frilly, incorrectly stored,

not guessing at what she would be thinking
later when the police showed up, the reporters at the door.

Maybe she should have used more probing words
over toast in the morning,

not used caffeine and work as excuses.
Maybe she should have tried to remember

that desire wasn't always something that flowed like cold syrup
on snowy mornings or that compasses and weathervanes

could still work, even if you didn't live on a farm somewhere.
Sometimes you know the letter is coming,

You know what it will say,
but you can't make the first incision in the envelope.

"Your uncle was sick and now he is dead.
You were his favorite. Please come."

But sometimes there is no writing, no return address,
no mark, just the normal square blind edges.

And you can run your fingers around the envelope
and open it up, wondering what the thing inside will tell you,

not knowing what delicate treasure you are about to unwrap,
what small message, red, folded, and still.

PAINTED ON A BARN

in large letters was the word PIG.
I could clearly read the word from the road.
There was nothing about "For sale" or "Farm."

What compulsion drove a man to label something so?
Did his wife have a special embroidered apron
with the word WOMAN emblazoned?

(Or, during those intimate hours,
did she have a girdle where her title would expand
horribly large in Lycra?)

Or maybe this was just a casual, derogatory remark
aimed at no one in particular, maybe just at God,
to express a fleeting state of mind, a heretofore repressed enmity?

Or maybe it was a warning, a desperate feeble attempt
to make us stay away, to keep driving,
to make us think, make us tremble,

to keep us away from the gnawed pen, the erupted door, the smell
of musky, muddy, crushed furniture, the hoof-scratched tiles,
the final red glimpse of a terrible porcine slop.

SKEFFINGTON'S DAUGHTER

Named after Sir Leonard Skeffington, its creator, this was the name given to a torture device housed in the Tower of London. It consisted of a hinged hoop in which victims were compelled to bend double, their legs against their chest. The hoop was then tightened until the victims confessed their crimes.

Love, I did not expect to see us here today.
Perhaps in a punt on the Thames,
yes, that would have worked:
Me, in a straw hat, dignified, slowly rowing;
You, with a shade, trailing your hand over the side.
But no, instead, I pictured us
in this stone room, in this woman's embrace.
What possessed me, what made me look
when others turned away?
The bitter sweetness of the gall that rose,
the discordant choir of phantoms,
all served to better form and focus on this progeny.
To be proud of a hoop, an endless ring:
What strange insemination could conjure up
such a tempered child
whose grim embrace does not relent?
Oh, love, what strange offspring
our desire has made around us,
making us breathless with need,
milling us flesh to flesh, binding us tight,
until we will become the perfect ring,
a true contour within a soundless world,
making us take ever shallower breaths,
the oblique light fading,
our love making us mute in our devotion,
when old age makes us totter,
bent like a prayer
by the pincers of God.

MOVING THE Peruvian Mummies

Into the cliff dwellings the archeologists climbed like arthritic monkeys. They
stirred the pot shards, dissembled old shawls, misinterpreted hieroglyphs.
They came with their questioning meters and their steaming, humid bodies.
They came, already tasting the heady, air-conditioned endorphins that would
come to their tongues when they stood in the crush outside the temperature-
controlled glass cases where the mummies would be moved. They took the
mummies that had presided unruffled in these caves for centuries. They
wrapped them like papooses and layered them with rags to catch each and every
decaying flake as the omnivorous air, held so long at bay, finally began to gnaw.
And when all the taut-skin bundles had been boxed then those archeologists
looked at each other with somehow different eyes, knowing they had lost their
pillaging virginity, and they justified it by saying, over and over, how nothing
can remain intact.

LINES UPON A TRANQUIL PAGE WHOSE NAME I CAN'T REMEMBER

I grew up on Bugs Bunny,
       and Elmer Fudd,
traces of Robert E. Howard,
       and Lovecraft,
    Bierce,
      Poe,
    Clark Ashton Smith.
      They all had a part.
Adam Strange
     and
     TA DA!

                    (superman!)

And sometimes now I imagine
      they live in my pen,
    and, occasionally,
   one of them will stir
     and step out
(in a different form)
   and smile at me
      from where's he landed
        with black india feet
           upon the page.

THE WIFE OF THE LUMBERJACK KING

would always sit in the audience
during the speed-chopping competition
and admire the way his outsized arms and shoulders
would almost burst the seams of the red flannel.
From the waist down he was scrawny, a stick,
but from the waist up, well,
tremulous, the way she would describe herself
to whomever was sitting close,
tremulous, with some fluttery on the side.
With chest flushed and eyes all liquid
she would be the first to applaud as he captured
another event.
Then she'd laugh ha-ha with joy and relief
and point out to whomever would listen
that good thing he was good with an axe
because he was lousy on a bicycle
and a teetering wreck on skates
with those bird legs and tiny feet.
What a good guffaw at that!
What a funny sight to imagine!

But that crowd's mind never extended as far as
those unsettling nights, nights after nights,
where he would have to always hold onto any wall for balance,
when he had to be careful not to trip on the cracks in the linoleum,
when she would lie awake at night
marveling and despairing on his tiny, tiny toes.

LIKE A BOLT

After the fourth time Love had come and gone
she quit asking herself if it was her, or if it was him,
or if she just had
lousy self-destructive choices in men.
She quit asking if it was a problem with commitment,
or a problem with her career, her dog, her car,
or where she was living.
But something had to be blamed
so she decided to lay it all on Planet X,
that big chunka rock she had read about
in the *Enquirer.*
Planet X, yessir, that asteroid that was gonna
smash kablooey into the Earth sometime next year.
When she was younger she used to laugh ha-ha
at those folks out in Roswell who would hold up signs that said,
"Aliens! Please try again! We are friendly!"
But she understood better now.
Sometimes you had to give in
and accept that there were forces
larger than you that just governed everything—
where you lived, where you worked, what you ate—
you had to quit struggling, you had to just go with
that vast pseudo-gravitational force that was, you hoped, making something rush
toward you.
So in a moment of sheer inspired madness,
she had gone and painted a big red HERE
on the roof of every one of her ex-lover's houses.
It might not make a difference, but it was simpler
than holding up a single welcoming sign.
And if it worked it would certainly level things out,
it would give things closure,
it would make things all right.

THE COUSIN WHO SAW THE UFO

pulled his story inside him
like a religion he had abandoned.

He told the story once,
let others pass it on,
finally denied it.

He grew circles under his eyes
like old potatoes, thick and puffy.
Sometimes he would get up in the middle of the night
and start and stop and start his car.

There was a tiny fear inside him now—
like buying a seed-pack
at the hardware store
waiting for geraniums
and something brown, ragged, and musky coming up.

It was like something that could fill a person
unexpectedly,
like when you were little,
staying up past the lightning bugs,
barefooted, in the yard,
the stars suddenly too deep,
your father's hand too far away.

It was like almost being asleep, your eyes shut,
seeing ghostly strings floating in your eyes.
and hearing muffled, against your pillow,
what might be your heartbeat
or not.

PINOCCHIO

It was probably when he learned to sing with real vocal cords
that he learned the true full losing extent
of what he had wished for and gained.
For while he was exactly a young boy,
with bursting ganglia and hormones suddenly afire,
his former wooden knots were old wood, thickly ringed,
and they had seen much.

So this was his voice then, he remembered asking.
Its fluttering hardly moved the leaves and could not stir the birds
who remembered him as timid branches they had once rested on.

He soon discovered that it is easy to be one thing, or the other,
but not both, that the wonder of faster corpuscles,
and the pleasurable burn of swift movement eventually fades.
He had forgotten: initials carved into a tree
are quickly outgrown, they moss over, people reach beyond them,
please don't remember them, that was a different me.

Now, still feeling like all big buttons and thick fingers,
he smoked another cigarette
because the burning irony delighted him.

He considered that when all things were weighed,
when the bowl was tipped over and the fish dissected,
why, he could read what the entrails said:
"This is what you wished for:
a gift from some small blue insignificant buzzing
that ultimately you could not swat away."
The pain in his worn, aging joints,
the burls and swirls of his fleshy ethereal hands,
his stiff and pointed nose (that he was told one day
would still continue to grow even after he died—
another joke he thought)—
this was vitality then. this grim fulfillment,
this inflicted gift that twisted his guts like roots.

He had been swallowed by a desire that would not heave him out.

He ground out his cigarette with a nubbed toe
while a thought clacked hollowly in his head:
how could he get that damning buzzing back
so he could ask for one more painful consummation,
that he might clip-clop his way to fulfill a pitiful yearning,
to be cradled in a final sleeping
on the breast of some dark Bavarian wood?

ROBERT FROST AMONG THE CANNIBALS

It came to me one evening at a reading
as my words fell at the feet of the crowd
that Robert Frost did not meet Death
as well as he might have.
Which is not to say that he did not meet it nobly.
That might have been so. No, I mean,
perhaps such a man,
so rich in language, so talented of tongue,
should perhaps have met his end
in some fatal last adventure
deep in a jungle, should have had his Nature
meet one final proofing,
one ultimate telling scansion.
Dying in bed? Now there's a benign ending.
But preaching a New England drawl to lost savages?
There is saint-like glory of sorts there,
regardless of whether
those aboriginals were less concerned about mending walls and
snowy woods
than how should they divide the portions
and how thick was his leg.
Imagine how after he had finished his recitation,
to show their appreciation,
those cannibals might have risen up
and consumed him whole, all parts, nothing wasted. And, finally,
            afterwards,
as they gnawed on his bones
and sucked his marrow for dessert,
they would pat their stretched bellies and say what we already knew,
"Who was that man?
The very meat of him was thin and stringy at best.
But oh! Didn't he speak well when he was still alive?"

WHERE ALL THINGS ARE FIXED

In accordance with what he believed,
when Ovid died he was transformed,
but, unexpectedly, it was into
a rogue piece of popcorn
dropped and now stale and wedged in
the old seat cushion of an art house movie theatre
over on sixth street where they showed classics
and foreign films with sub-titles.

This is only a short tale with deep repercussions.
In brief, Ovid discovered that all philosophies have boundaries
and he been placed in the middle of both the
reality and refutation of his.
He also discovered that there was probably no one
more beautiful and ageless in the world than Nora Charles.
How he longed to hold her, to light her cigarette,
to make her a special martini (whatever those things were,
in or out of context, he would do them).
But he was only popcorn after all
with limited sentience and logical thought.
This next time through the story, he thought,
this story that never alters in the least,
Nora will notice me instead of Nick
and we will change together into something
together, something powerful and majestic.
two twining oaks perhaps.

I will wait right here, he thought,
until she looks.

VINCENT VAN GOGH RODE WITH LBJ ONE DAY

in that Texan's convertible
as it tore its high compressioned and
shock-ruined way across the wild Texas hill country.
There would have been nothing in France
that Vincent could have compared it with, of course.
Absolutely nothing like the wild, bouncing, turf-tearing
circular turns that sent cactus exploding
into juicy spiked green swirls,
nothing like those moments
of charging into wildflowers like a mad bull,
his shoulders getting bathed
with showers of fiery Indian blanket
and clouds of bluebonnets that were a darker azure
                    than any night he had ever imagined.
He tried screaming once
But the roar of the V-8 drowned him out.
It's a dream I will wake up from, Vincent thought,
as he clung with white knuckles to the dashboard,
his desperate eyes searching for any sign of culture
but instead only seeing
                  rattlesnakes striking at the tires.
It is a nightmare where I am kidnapped
        by a demonic, big-nosed madman.
I am actually sleeping in my loft beside the Seine,
contemplating in my slumber how I shall
            angrily paint angst—
then Whoosh!
                a sudden right turn to avoid a burr oak
                and Vincent found himself chewing
                some pretty close to reality upholstery.
Oh, little did poor Vincent know
that even then that larger-than-life-President
was looking over at his passenger
and wondering if he could shake
        some sanity and courage into him
if he reached over and grabbed him
by his one remaining ear.

SETTING ONESELF ON FIRE

Rumor has it that Joan of Arc,
somewhere in that gap of time between
exoneration and being burned at the stake,
was made immortal
and she is now living in the housing district in Chicago
drawing erotic cartoons
about Hispanics and African Americans.
If you find her and ask her she will tell you everything:
her name, where she is from, where she has lived.
She will confess it all.
"I simply walked away," she will tell you.
"The ropes burned off. I simply walked away.
People saw what they wanted to see
and then they quit listening.
I have tried to find
other ways."
She will tilt her head to one side,
And consider your next question.
"A saint? Well, I have visited Mount Sauvage, twice,
and both times it was lit by St. Elmo's fire
but I was the only one who saw it.
Does that make me a saint?
I think not. And Holy?
No, no. Leave the idea of holy mountains, of holy persons,
of holy places, of holy nations, behind you."
She will laugh at your stammer.
"There is, how do you say it, transubstantiation,
in every second. That is the message that was lost.
Seeing that does not make me a saint.
But saying that evidently does.
Now, please, the light, it is failing …,"
then she will fall back into archaic French, mumbling between her
perfect pursed lips,
"It is not about the flesh.
It is all about the flesh. It always was."
She will sigh, reach for a new nub for her pen,
and try to get a certain exposed breast
exactly right.

ACKNOWLEDGMENTS

Borderlands for "You Should Be Here, Marianne Moore"

Concho River Review for "When The Big Rains Came"

Encore for "Poetry, Right Here, In The Chute"

Grasslands Review for "On The Path To The Mayan Pyramid," "The Separation of the Seasons"

Ilya's Honey for "The Former Poet Laureate Said," "John The Baptist's Head"

Langdon Review for "A Bowl," "Like A Bolt," "Like The Mother Finding Her Daughter's Baby In A Drawer," "Pinocchio," "Robert Frost Among the Cannibals," "Skeffington's Daughter," "The Man Who Didn't Mean To Take Away My Faith," "Vincent Van Gogh Rode with LBJ One Day," "The Wife Of The Lumberjack King," "Where All Things Are Fixed"

New Texas for "El Dia Del Muerte," "Moving The Peruvian Mummies," "Setting Oneself on Fire"

Poet's Forum Magazine for "A Painting Of A Blacksmith"

The Poetry Victims for "Bewitched"

Shadow of the Green Fuse for "Lines Upon A Tranquil Page Whose Name I Don't Remember"

Spiky Palm for "Drifting"

Suddenly for "Wet Water," "Like Rat-Tat-Tat-Marching Clockwork, Pacific, Central, or Greenwich Mean"

Texas in Poetry 2 for "Coronado Points"

Several of these poems appeared in the previous volumes *Bone Song*, *Weighed in the Balances*, and *No Boundaries*.

In addition, several of these poems appeared in various yearbooks of The Poetry Society of Texas.